A Check List Of Indiana Mollusca: With Localities

L. E. Daniels

In the interest of creating a more extensive selection of rare historical book reprints, we have chosen to reproduce this title even though it may possibly have occasional imperfections such as missing and blurred pages, missing text, poor pictures, markings, dark backgrounds and other reproduction issues beyond our control. Because this work is culturally important, we have made it available as a part of our commitment to protecting, preserving and promoting the world's literature. Thank you for your understanding.

A CHECK LIST OF INDIANA MOLLUSCA, WITH LOCALITIES.

By L. E. Daniels.

The following is a list of the Mollusca with localities which were known to occur in Indiana on January 1, 1903, 276 species in all. The nomenclature of the land shells is that of Pilsbry's catalogue, mentioned in the introduction to the preceding paper. That of the Unionidæ is Simpson's "Synopsis of the Naiades, or Pearly Fresh Water Mussels," published in Vol. XXII of the Proceedings of the U. S. National Museum. Where the name used in Call's "Catalogue of the Mollusca of Indiana" differs from that of the present list, Call's name follows in italics and in parenthesis. Representatives of all but a half dozen of the species are in the State Museum.

Family HELICIDÆ.

Sub-family HELICINÆ.

1. VALLONIA PULCHELLA (Mull.).

    Indianapolis, Mitchell and Arlington; common in southeastern Indiana.

2. VALLONIA COSTATA (Mull.).

    Arlington, Marshall County.

Sub-family POLYGYRINÆ.

3. POLYGYRA LEPORINA (Gld.).

    New Harmony, Posey County; North Vernon, Jennings County; Dunreith, Henry County (Pleas.); Gibson County (Stein).

4. POLYGYRA PLICATA Say.

    Clarksville, Floyd County.

5. POLYGYRA TRIDENTATA (Say). (*Triodopsis tridentata* Say).

    Found all over the State.

6. POLYGYRA FRAUDULENTA Pils. (*Triodopsis fallax* Say).
   Not *Polygyra fallax* (Say), which is an eastern species, according to Pilsbry.
   Mt. Vernon, Lafayette, Laporte and Indianapolis.

7. POLYGYRA INFLECTA Say. (*Triodopsis inflecta* Say).
   Abundant in nearly all parts of the State.

8. POLYGYRA PROFUNDA (Say). (*Mesodon profundus* Say).
   Indianapolis, Corydon, Lawrenceburg, Brookville, Lower Wabash Valley.

9. POLYGYRA ALBOLABRIS (Say.) (*Mesodon albolabris* Say).
   All over the State.

10. POLYGYRA EXOLETA (Binn). (*Mesodon exoletus* Binn.)
    Common over the southern two-thirds of the State.

11. POLYGYRA MULTILINEATA (Say). (*Mesodon multilineatus* Say).
    All over the State in suitable localities.

12. POLYGYRA PALLIATA (Say). (*Triodopsis palliata* Say).
    All over the State.

13. POLYGYRA OBSTRICTA (Say). (*Triodopsis obstricta* Say).
    Grand Chain and New Harmony, Posey County.

14. POLYGYRA APPRESSA (Say). (*Triodopsis appressa* Say).
    New Harmony, Mt. Vernon, Lawrenceburg, Cannelton and Wyandotte.

15. POLYGYRA ELEVATA (Say). (*Mesodon elevatus* Say).
    All over the State.

16. POLYGYRA PENNSYLVANICA (Green). (*Mesodon pennsylvanicus* Green).
    Brookville, Lafayette and Brookston.

17. POLYGYRA THYROIDES (Say). (*Mesodon thyroideus* Say).
    All over the State.

18. POLYGYRA CLAUSA (Say). (*Mesodon clausus* Say).
    Brookville, Lafayette, De Long. Over nearly all of the State.

19. POLYGYRA MITCHELLIANA (Lea). (*Mesodon mitchellianus* Lea).
    Brookville.

20. POLYGYRA STENOTREMA (Fer.). (*Stenotrema stenotremum* Fer.).
    Madison, Lawrenceburg; common at Wyandotte.

21. POLYGYRA HIRSUTA (Say). (*Stenotrema hirsutum* Say).
    All over the State.

22. POLYGYRA MONODON (Fack.). (*Stenotrema leaii* Ward).
    Arlington, Marshall County; Pine and Hammond, Lake County; Rochester; near the lakes in Kosciusko and Steuben counties.

22a. P. MONODON FRATERNA (Say). (*Stenotrema monodon* Rack.).
    All over the State.

Family PUPIDÆ.

23. STROBILOPS LABYRINTHICA (Say). (*Strobila labyrinthica* Say).
    Brookville, North Vernon, Princeton, Huntingburg, Cannelton; New Harmony, Posey County; cypress swamps, Knox County.

24. STROBILOPS VIRGO (Pils.).
    Cannelton, New Harmony, Arlington, Princeton and Wyandotte.

25. STROBILOPS AFFINIS Pils.
    Lawrenceburg, Mitchell, Wyandotte; New Harmony, Posey County; Cannelton, Perry County; Huntingburg; near Lake James, Steuben County, and Tippecanoe Lake, Kosciusko County.

26. PUPOIDES MARGINATUS (Say). (*Leucochila fallax* Say).
    Brookville, North Vernon, Mitchell, New Harmony, Arlington and Pine. Dunreith (Pleas).

27. BIFIDARIA ARMIFERA Say. (*Leucochila armifera* Say).
    Brookville, Lawrenceburg, Mitchell, New Harmony, Arlington, Seymour and Indianapolis.

28. BIFIDARIA CONTRACTA Say. (*Leucochila contracta* Say).
    Vawter Park, Arlington, Brookville, Huntingburg, Indianapolis, North Vernon, Seymour, Mitchell and New Harmony.

29. BIFIDARIA PROCERA Gld.
    Mitchell, Connersville (Walker).

30. BIFIDARIA CORTICARIA (Say). (*Leucochila corticaria* Say).
    Grand Chain, New Harmony; Morgan County. Dunreith (Pleas).

31. BIFIDARIA HOLZINGERI Sterki.

    Dunreith (Sterki).

32. BIFIDARIA CURVIDENS Gld.

    Wolf Lake, Lake County (Baker); Henry County and Connersville (Sterki). Dunreith (Pleas).

33. BIFIDARIA PENTODON Say. (*Pupilla pentodon* Say).

    Tippecanoe and Turkey lakes, Kosciusko County, New Harmony, Mitchell, Arlington, Seymour. Dunreith (Pleas).

34. VERTIGO MILIUM Gld.

    Lake James, Steuben County; Vawter Park, Brookville and Lawrenceburg (Call). Dunreith (Pleas).

35. VERTIGO OVATA Say.

    Tippecanoe Lake, Kosciusko County; Lake James, Steuben County; Arlington. Dunreith (Pleas). Lawrenceburg and Indianapolis (Call).

36. VERTIGO MORSEI Sterki.

    Near Tippecanoe Lake, Kosciusko County; Lake Maxinkuckee, Marshall County, and Lake James, Steuben County.

37. VERTIGO GOULDI Binn.

    Henry County and Connersville (Sterki); Dunreith (Pleas).

38. VERTIGO TRIDENTATA Wolf.

    Danville (Walker); Dunreith (Pleas).

Family ACHATINIDÆ.

39. COCHLICOPA LUBRICA (Mull.). (*Fcrussacia subcylindrica* Linn.).

    New Harmony, Indianapolis, Wolf Lake, Lake County (Baker); northern half of the State (Call).

Family CIRCINARIIDÆ Pilsbry.

40. CIRCINARIA CONCAVA (Say). (*Macrocyclis concava* Say).

    All over the State.

Family ZONITIDÆ.

Sub-family ZONITINÆ Pilsbry.

41. OMPHALINA FULIGINOSA (Griff.). (*Zonites fuliginosus* Griff.).
    Grand Chain, Posey County; Mitchell and Wyandotte; Dunreith (Pleas); Corydon, Madison and Bloomington (Call).

42. OMPHALINA FRIABILIS (W. G. B.). (*Zonites friabilis* W. G. B.).
    Cypress swamps, Knox County.

43. OMPHALINA LÆVIGATA (Pfr.).
    Grand Chain and Mt. Vernon, Posey County; Cannelton and Laurel.

44. OMPHALINA INORNATA (Say). (*Zonites inornatus* Say).
    Laurel, Corydon, Madison and Lawrenceburg (Call).

45. VITREA CELLARIA (Mull.)
    Laporte (in greenhouse).

46. VITREA HAMMONIS (Strom.).
    Laurel, Indianapolis, Arlington, De Long, Vawter Park; Lake James, Steuben County, and cypress swamps, Knox County.

47. VITREA WHEATLEYI (Bland).
    New Harmony, Brookville, Huntingburg and Indianapolis.

48. VITREA INDENTATA Say.
    Cannelton, New Harmony, Mitchell, Indianapolis, Arlington, Brookville, North Vernon, Wyandotte, Seymour, Millers, Lawrenceburg and cypress swamps, Knox County.

49. VITREA CAPSELLA (Gld.).
    New Harmony, Posey County; and Huntingburg, Dubois County.

50. EUCONULUS FULVUS (Mull.). (*Zonites fulvus* Drap.).
    Arlington, Brookville, North Webster; Lake James, Steuben County, and Tippecanoe Lake, Kosciusko County.

51. EUCONULUS CHERSINUS Say.
    New Harmony, North Vernon, Huntingburg; Pine, Lake County; Morgan County, and cypress swamps, Knox County.

Sub-family ARIOPHANTINÆ Pilsbry.

52. ZONITOIDES NITIDUS (Mull.).

 Vawter Park, Tippecanoe Lake and North Webster, Kosciusko County; Arlington and De Long, Marshall County; Lake James, Steuben County.

53. ZONITOIDES ARBOREUS (Say). (*Zonites arboreus* Say).

 All over the State.

54. ZONITOIDES LIMATULUS (Ward). (*Zonites limatulus* Ward).

 Seymour and Indianapolis. Wabash and Terre Haute (Call).

55. ZONITOIDES MINUSCULUS (Binn.).

 Wolf Lake, Lake County (Baker); Mitchell, Huntingburg, Grand Chain, Seymour and Vawter Park.

56. ZONITOIDES LÆVISCULUS (Sterki).

 Dunreith, Henry County.

57. ZONITOIDES MILIUM (Morse).

 Princeton, Gibson County.

58. GASTRODONTA INTERTEXTA (Binn.). (*Zonites intertextus* Binn.).

 Grand Chain and Mt. Vernon, Posey County; Mitchell, Wyandotte; southeastern Indiana (Call).

59. GASTRODONTA DEMISSA (Binn.).

 Wolf Lake, Lake County (Baker).

60. GASTRODONTA LIGERA (Say). (*Zonites ligerus* Say).

 Grand Chain and New Harmony, Posey County.

61. GASTRODONTA INTERNA (Say). (*Zonites internus* Say).

 Cannelton and Wyandotte.

Family LIMACIDÆ.

62. LIMAX FLAVUS L.

 Lawrenceburg (Call).

63. AGRIOLIMAX AGRESTIS (L.).

 Laporte County.

64. AGRIOLIMAX CAMPESTRIS (Binn.).

 Common.

Family PHILOMYCIDÆ.

65. PHILOMYCUS CAROLINENSIS (Bosc.). (*Tebennophorus carolinensis* Bosc.).
    Over nearly all the State.

Family ENDODONTIDÆ.

66. PYRAMIDULA ALTERNATA (Say). (*Patula alternata* Say).
    All over the State.

67. PYRAMIDULA SOLITARIA (Say). (*Patula solitaria* Say).
    Lafayette, Laporte, Terre Haute, New Harmony, Mt. Vernon, Lawrenceburg, North Vernon, Vawter Park.

68. PYRAMIDULA PERSPECTIVA (Say). (*Patula perspectiva* Say).
    All over the State.

69. PYRAMIDULA STRIATELLA (Anth.). (*Patula striatella* Anth.).
    Indianapolis, Brookville, Lawrenceburg, Corydon, Lafayette.

70. HELICODISCUS LINEATUS (Say).
    Seymour, Huntingburg, North Vernon, New Harmony, Vawter Park, Lafayette and Indianapolis.

Sub-family PUNCTINÆ.

71. PUNCTUM PYGMÆUM (Drap.).
    Seymour, Jackson County, and Vawter Park, Kosciusko County.

72. SPHYRADIUM EDENTULUM (Drap.).
    Near Clear Lake, Steuben County, and Vawter Park, Kosciusko County.

Family SUCCINIDÆ.

73. SUCCINEA RETUSA Lea. (*Succinea ovalis* Gld.).
    Kosciusko, Marshall, Laporte, Steuben and Lake counties.

74. SUCCINEA CALUMETENSIS Calkins.
    Half Moon Pond, Posey County, and cypress swamps, Knox County.

75. SUCCINEA OVALIS Say. (*Succinea obliqua* Say).
    Arlington and De Long, Fulton County.

76. SUCCINEA AVARA Say.
    Kosciusko, Laporte and Whitley counties.

Family AURICULIDÆ.

77. CARYCHIUM EXIGUUM Say.

Tippecanoe Lake and Vawter Park, Kosciusko County; Lawrenceburg, New Albany and Indianapolis (Call).

78. CARYCHIUM EXILE H. C. Lea.

Vawter Park, Kosciusko County; Berry Lake, Lake County (Baker).

Family LIMNÆIDÆ.

Sub-family LIMNÆINÆ.

79. LIMNÆA STAGNALIS APPRESSA Say.

Turkey Lake, Kosciusko County; Lake Michigan, Millers; Kankakee River, Laporte County.

80. LIMNÆA REFLEXA Say. (*Limnophysa reflexa* Say).

Hammond, Millers, near Lake Michigan; Kankakee River, Laporte County. Common in northern Indiana.

80a. L. REFLEXA KIRTLANDIANA Lea.

Roby, Lake County.

81. LIMNÆA PALUSTRIS Mull. (*Limnophysa palustris* Mull.).

Turkey and Tippecanoe lakes, Kosciusko County; Carr's Slough, White County, and cypress swamps, Knox County.

81a. L. PALUSTRIS MICHIGANENSIS Walker.

Tippecanoe and Turkey lakes, Kosciusko County; Calumet Lake, Lake County (Baker).

82. LIMNÆA CAPERATA Say. (*Limnophysa caperata* Say).

Hammond, North Vernon, Calumet Lake and Roby (Baker).

82a. L. CAPERATA UMBILICATA Adams.

Liverpool, Lake County (Baker).

83. LIMNÆA CATASCOPIUM Say.

Calumet Lake, Lake County (Baker).

84. LIMNÆA COLUMELLA Say.

Bass Lake, Starke County; Grassy Creek, Kosciusko County.

85. LIMNÆA WOODRUFFI Baker.

Lake Michigan at Pine, Millers and Michigan City.

CHECK LIST OF INDIANA MOLLUSCA. 637

86. LIMNÆA HUMILIS Say. (*Limnophysa humilis* Say).

    Turkey and Tippecanoe lakes, Kosciusko County; Bass Lake, Starke County; Round Lake, Whitley County, and Lake Maxinkuckee, Marshall County.

87. LIMNÆA DESIDIOSA Say. (*Limnophysa desidiosa* Say).

    Grassy Creek, Kosciusko County. All over the State (Call).

Sub-family PLANORBINÆ.

88. PLANORBIS TRIVOLVIS Say. (*Helisoma trivolvis* Say).

    All over the State.

89. PLANORBIS TRUNCATUS Miles.

    George Lake, Lake County (T. Jenson).

90. PLANORBIS BICARINATUS Say. (*Helisoma bicarinata* Say).

    Lake Michigan, Michigan City; Lake James, Steuben County; Bass Lake, Starke County; Clear Lake, Laporte County.

91. PLANORBIS CAMPANULATUS Say. (*Planorbella campanulata* Say).

    Common over the northern part of the State.

92. PLANORBIS EXACUTUS Say. (*Menetus exacutus* Say).

    Bass Lake, Starke County; Turkey Lake and Grassy Creek, Kosciusko County; Cedar Lake, Lake County; Lawrenceburg and Ft. Wayne (Call).

93. PLANORBIS PARVUS Say. (*Gyraulus parvus* Say).

    Bass Lake, Starke County; Lake Maxinkuckee, Marshall County; Cedar Lake, Lake County; Lake James, Steuben County; Grassy Creek, Kosciusko County, and Pine Lake, Lake County.

93a. P. PARVUS CIRCUMSTRIATUS Tyron.

    Lake Maxinkuckee, Marshall County.

94. PLANORBIS HIRSUTUS Gld.

    Grassy Creek, Tippecanoe Lake and Turkey Lake, Kosciusko County; Cedar Lake, Lake County; Bass Lake, Starke County.

95. PLANORBIS DEFLECTUS Say. (*Gyraulus deflectus* Say).

    Grassy Creek, Kosciusko County.

96. PLANORBIS UMBILICATELLUS Cockerell.

    Tippecanoe Lake, Kosciusko County.

97. SEGMENTINA ARMIGERA Say.

Carr's Slough, White County; cypress swamps, Knox County; Turkey and Tippecanoe lakes, Kosciusko County; Lake Maxinkuckee, Marshall County; Lake James, Steuben County.

Family ANCYLIDÆ.

98. ANCYLUS RIVULARIS Say.

Bass Lake, Starke County; Liverpool, Lake County (Baker).

99. ANCYLUS PARALLELUS Hald.

Bass Lake, Starke County.

100. ANCYLUS SHIMEKII Pils.

Bass Lake, Starke County.

101. ANCYLUS FUSCUS Adams.

Grassy Creek, Kosciusko County.

102. ANCYLUS DIAPHANUS Hald.

In State Museum, marked Indiana.

103. ANCYLUS TARDUS Say.

Grassy Creek, Kosciusko County; Ohio River, Lawrenceburg; Wabash and Maumee rivers (Call).

Family PHYSIDÆ.

104. PHYSA HETEROSTROPHA Say.

New Harmony, Posey County; Tippecanoe and Turkey lakes, Kosciusko County.

105. PHYSA ANCILLARIA Say.

Logansport; Collection Indiana State University from Turkey Lake, Kosciusko County (Call).

106. PHYSA SAYI Toppan.

Turkey and Tippecanoe lakes, Kosciusko County.

107. PHYSA RHOMBOIDEA Crandall.

Cypress swamps, Knox County.

108. PHYSA GYRINA Say.

New Harmony, Wyandotte, Indianapolis, cypress swamps, Knox County.

109. P. GYRINA ELLIPTICA Lea.

Cypress swamps, Knox County.

110. PHYSA INTEGRA Hald.

Wyandotte; Lake Michigan at Michigan City.

111. APLEXA HYPNORUM Linn. (*Bulinus hypnorum* Linn.).

Tippecanoe Lake and Vawter Park, Kosciusko County; Hammond, Lake County; Brookston, White County.

Family PLEUROCERIDÆ.

112. LITHASIA OBOVATA Say.

Falls of the Ohio River; Lawrenceburg (Call).

112a. L. OBOVATA BICONICA Pilsbry.

Wabash River, Gibson County.

113. ANGITREMA ARMIGERA Say.

Wabash River, Grand Chain, Posey County; Knox County. Common.

114. ANGITREMA VERRUCOSA Raf.

Wabash River, New Harmony, common; Ohio River, Lawrenceburg (A. C. Billups).

115. PLEUROCERA UNDULATUM Say.

Wabash River, Gibson and Posey counties. Common.

116. PLEUROCERA MONILIFERUM Lea.

Wabash River, Gibson County.

117. PLEUROCERA CANALICULATUM Say.

Wabash River, Gibson and Posey counties; Ohio River, New Albany.

118. PLEUROCERA SUBULARE Lea.

Manitou Lake, Rochester; Tippecanoe Lake, Kosciusko County; Wabash River, Terre Haute; Eel River, North Manchester.

119. PLEUROCERA ELEVATUM Say.

Ohio River at "The Falls" and Lawrenceburg.

120. PLEUROCERA ALVEARE Conrad.

Wabash River, Gibson County.

121. GONIOBASIS CUBICOIDES Anthony.

 Blue River, Wyandotte; Big Indian Creek, Corydon; Wabash River, Huntington (Call).

122. GONIOBASIS DEPYGIS Say.

 Falls of the Ohio. Specimens in State Museum marked Wabash River.

123. GONIOBASIS LIVESCENS Menke.

 Lake Maxinkuckee, Marshall County; Bass Lake, Starke County; St. Mary's and Maumee and Ft. Wayne (Call).

124. GONIOBASIS INFANTULA Lea.

 Falls of the Ohio near Shippingport (Call).

125. GONIOBASIS PULCHELLA Anthony.

 Big Indian Creek, Corydon; Blue River, Wyandotte; White River, Indianapolis.

126. GONIOBASIS INTERLINEATA Anthony.

 Christy Creek, type locality.

127. GONIOBASIS INTERSITA Hald.

 Swan Creek, type locality (Mrs. Say).

128. GONIOBASIS SEMICARINATA Say.

 Small streams flowing from Hamer's Cave at Mitchell; Muscatatuck River, North Vernon.

129. GONIOBASIS LOUISVILLENSIS Lea.

 Falls of the Ohio.

130. GONIOBASIS GRACILIOR Anthony.

 Turkey Lake, Kosciusko County; Manitou Lake, Rochester.

131. GONIOBASIS BREVISPIRA Anthony.

 Tippecanoe River, Carroll County; Sharp's Spring, Wyandotte.

132. GONIOBASIS INDIANENSIS Pilsbry.

 Blue River, Wyandotte, Crawford County.

133. ANCULOSA COSTATA Anthony.

 Ohio River, New Albany.

134. ANCULOSA TRILINEATA Say.

Ohio River, Lawrenceburg. Described from the Falls of the Ohio.

135. ANCULOSA PRÆROSA Say.

Ohio River, Lawrenceburg; Falls of the Ohio. Common.

Family AMNICOLIDÆ.

Sub-family BYTHINIINÆ.

136. BYTHINIA TENTACULATA Linne.

Lake Michigan at Pine, Millers and Michigan City.

Sub-family HYDROBIINÆ.

137. AMNICOLA LIMOSA Say.

Lake Michigan, Michigan City; Bass Lake, Starke County; Tippecanoe Lake, Kosciusko County; Cedar Lake, Lake County.

137a. A. LIMOSA PARVA Lea.

Turkey and Tippecanoe lakes, Kosciusko County; Bass Lake, Starke County.

137b. A. LIMOSA PORATA Say. (*Amnicola porata* Say).

Tippecanoe Lake, Kosciusko County; Bass Lake, Starke County.

138. AMNICOLA LUSTRICA Pils.

Turkey and Tippecanoe lakes, Kosciusko County; Lake Maxinkuckee, Marshall County; Berry Lake, Lake County (Baker).

139. AMNICOLA WALKERI Pils.

Grassy Creek, Kosciusko County.

140. AMNICOLA CINCINNATIENSIS Anthony.

Lake Michigan at Millers.

141. AMNICOLA EMARGINATA Kuster. (*Bythinella obtusa* Lea).

Lake Michigan at Millers.

142. PALUDESTRINA NICKLINIANA Lea.

Berry Lake, Lake County.

143. SOMATOGYRUS SUBGLOBOSUS Say. (*Somatogyrus isogonus* Say).

Ohio River, Lawrenceburg; George Lake, Lake County (Baker).

144. SOMATOGYRUS INTEGER Say.

Ohio River near Madison; Ohio River, Charleston (Call).

145. POMATIOPSIS LAPIDARIA Say.

Indianapolis, Seymour, Lawrenceburg, Calumet Lake, Lake County.

Family VALVATIDÆ.

146. VALVATA SINCERA Say.

Lake Michigan, Millers and Michigan City.

147. VALVATA TRICARINATA Say.

Lake Michigan at Millers; Grassy Creek, Kosciusko County; Lake James, Steuben County; Lake Maxinkuckee, Marshall County; Cedar Lake, Lake County.

147a. V. TRICARINATA CONFUSA Walker.

147b. V. TRICARINATA UNICARINATA De Kay.

147c. V. TRICARINATA SIMPLEX Gld.

Cedar Lake, Lake County.

148. VALVATA BICARINATA Lea.

Lake Michigan.

148a. V. BICARINATA NORMALIS Walker.

Lake Michigan, Millers.

Family VIVIPARIDÆ.

149. VIVIPARA SUBPURPUREA Say.

Wabash River, Grand Chain, Posey County; Big Creek and Hovey's Lake, Posey County; Wabash River, Knox County; Ohio River, Mt. Vernon.

150. VIVIPARA CONTECTOIDES Binney.

Bass Lake, Starke County; Foote's Pond, Gibson County; Dan's Pond, Knox County; Lake Michigan, Millers.

151. VIVIPARA INTERTEXTA Say.

Cypress swamps, Knox County; Wabash River, Knox and Gibson counties.

152. CAMPELOMA PONDEROSUM Say.

Wabash River, Lafayette, Terre Haute, New Harmony; Ohio River, Mt. Vernon; Muscatatuck River, North Vernon.

153. CAMPELOMA SUBSOLIDUM Anthony.

Wabash River, Lafayette, Terre Haute; Kankakee River, Riverside; Eel River, North Manchester.

154. CAMPELOMA DECISUM Say.

Bass Lake, Starke County; Kankakee, St. Mary's, St. Joseph and Maumee rivers (Call).

155. CAMPELOMA RUFUM Hald.

Tippecanoe and Turkey lakes, Kosciusko County; Pine and Stone lakes, Laporte County; Lake Michigan, Millers. Lafayette, Indianapolis, Huntington and Ft. Wayne (Call).

156. CAMPELOMA INTEGRUM De Kay.

Webster Lake, Kosciusko County; Clear Lake, Steuben County; Lake Michigan, Millers.

157. CAMPELOMA OBESA Lewis.

White River and Canal at Indianapolis.

158. LIOPLAX SUBCARINATA Say.

Wabash River, Grand Chain, Posey County; White, Ohio and Blue rivers (Call).

Family SPHÆRIIDÆ.

159. SPHÆRIUM VERMONTANUM Prime.

Lake Michigan, Millers.

160. SPHÆRIUM SOLIDULUM Prime.

Muscatatuck River, North Vernon.

161. SPHÆRIUM STAMINEUM Con.

White River, Indianapolis; Muscatatuck River, North Vernon; Lake Michigan, Michigan City; Tippecanoe and Turkey lakes, Kosciusko County.

162. SPHÆRIUM STRIATINUM Lam.

Tippecanoe Lake, Kosciusko County; Muscatatuck River, North Vernon; Corydon.

163. SPHÆRIUM SIMILE Say. (*Sphærium sulcatum* Lam.).

Turkey Lake, Kosciusko County; Lake Maxinkuckee, Marshall County; Wabash River, New Harmony.

164. SPHÆRIUM FABALE Prime.

Lake Michigan, Michigan City; Wabash River, New Harmony.

165. SPHÆRIUM OCCIDENTALE Prime.

Kankakee River, Laporte County; cypress swamps, Knox County; Tippecanoe Lake and pond at Vawter Park, Kosciusko County.

166. SPHÆRIUM RHOMBOIDEUM Say.

Turkey Lake, Kosciusko County; Lake Michigan at Millers.

167. SPHÆRIUM FLAVUM Prime.

Turkey Lake, Kosciusko County; variety from Lake Michigan at Millers.

168 CALYCULINA TRANSVERSA Say. (*Sphærium transversum* Say.)

Big Creek, Posey County; Wabash River, New Harmony.

169. CALYCULINA TRUNCATA Linsley.

Turkey and Tippecanoe lakes, Kosciusko County.

170. CALYCULINA SECURIS Prime.

Grassy Creek, Tippecanoe and Turkey lakes, Kosciusko County.

171. CALYCULINA PARTUMEIA Say. (*Sphærium partumeium* Say).

Grassy Creek, Kosciusko County.

172. CALYCULINA ROSACEA Prime.

Grassy Creek and Turkey Lake, Kosciusko County.

173. PISIDIUM ABDITUM Hald.

Berry Lake and Millers (Baker); Ohio and Wabash rivers, Brookville (Call).

174. PISIDIUM VIRGINICUM Bourg.

English Lake, Kankakee River.

175. PISIDIUM ROTUNDATUM Prime.

Grassy Creek, Tippecanoe and Turkey lakes, Kosciusko County.

176. PISIDIUM COMPRESSUM Prime.
   Grassy Creek and Turkey Lake, Kosciusko County; Bass Lake, Starke County; Lake Maxinkuckee, Marshall County; Kankakee River and Danville.

177. PISIDIUM DANIELSI Sterki (Ms.).
   Spring near Lake James, Steuben County.

178. PISIDIUM OBTUSALE C. Pfr.
   Spring near Lake James, Steuben County.

179. PISIDIUM NOV-EBORACENSE Prime.
   Grassy Creek and Turkey Lake, Kosciusko County; Bass Lake, Starke County.

180. PISIDIUM VARIABILE Prime.
   Bass Lake, Starke County; Turkey Lake, Kosciusko County; Lake Maxinkuckee, Marshall County; English Lake, Kankakee River.

181. PISIDIUM IDAHOENSE Roper.
   Lake Michigan, Millers.

182. PISIDIUM POLITUM Sterki.
   Grassy Creek, Kosciusko County.

183. PISIDIUM VESICULARE Sterki.
   Bass Lake, Starke County.

184. PISIDIUM PAUPERCULUM Sterki.
   Lake Maxinkuckee, Marshall County; Bass Lake, Starke County; Turkey Lake, Kosciusko County.

185. PISIDIUM SCUTELLATUM Sterki.
   Lost Lake, Marshall County.

186. PISIDIUM SPLENDIDULUM Sterki.
   Grassy Creek and Turkey Lake, Kosciusko County; Bass Lake, Starke County.

187. PISIDIUM ROPERI Sterki.
   Grassy Creek and Tippecanoe Lake, Kosciusko County; Danville (Sterki).

188. PISIDIUM MEDIANUM Sterki.
   Bass Lake, Starke County.

189. PISIDIUM TENUISSIMUM Sterki.
    Bass Lake, Starke County; Lake Maxinkuckee, Marshall County.

190. PISIDIUM AFFINE Sterki.
    Turkey Lake, Kosciusko County.

191. PISIDIUM SARGENTI Sterki.
    Bass Lake, Starke County.

192. PISIDIUM STRENGI Sterki.
    Bass Lake, Starke County.

193. PISIDIUM KIRKLANDI Sterki.
    Berry Lake, Lake County (Baker).

Family UNIONIDÆ.

194. TRUNCILLA TRIQUETRA Raf. (*Unio triangularis* Barnes).
    Tippecanoe, Wabash, Blue, White, Muscatatuck and Eel rivers.

195. TRUNCILLA SULCATA Lea. (*Unio sulcatus* Lea).
    Wabash River, Lafayette; White River, Marion County, Ohio River (Stein).

196. TRUNCILLA FOLIATA Hild. (*Unio foliatus* Hild.).
    Ohio and Wabash rivers (Stein).

197. TRUNCILLA PERSONATA Say. (*Unio personatus* Say).
    Wabash River, New Harmony. Authentic specimen in State Museum.

198. TRUNCILLA PERPLEXA Lea. (*Unio perplexus* Lea).
    Wabash River, New Harmony; Ohio River (Stein).

198a. T. PERPLEXA RANGIANA Lea.
    Wabash River, Lafayette; Tippecanoe River, Monticello; White River (Stein).

199. TRUNCILLA SAMPSONII Lea.
    Wabash River; Grand Chain, Posey County.

200. MICROMYA FABALIS Lea. (*Unio fabalis* Lea).
    White, Wabash and Tippecanoe rivers; Tippecanoe Lake, Kosciusko County.

CHECK LIST OF INDIANA MOLLUSCA.

201. LAMPSILIS VENTRICOSUS Barnes. (*Unio ventricosus* Barnes; *Unio subovatus* Say).
    Common all over the State.

202. LAMPSILIS CAPAX Green. (*Unio capax* Green).
    Wabash River, New Harmony and Grand Chain; Ohio River.

203. LAMPSILIS OVATUS Say.
    Wabash River, Terre Haute, Lafayette; Ohio River.

204. LAMPSILIS MULTIRADIATUS Lea. (*Unio multiradiatus* Lea).
    Wabash, Tippecanoe, Blue, White, Eel and Ohio rivers; Tippecanoe Lake. Common.

205. LAMPSILIS LUTEOLUS Lam. (*Unio luteolus* Lam.).
    Common all over the State.

206. LAMPSILIS LIGAMENTINUS Lam. (*Unio ligamentinus* Lam.).
    Common all over the State.

207. LAMPSILIS ORBICULATUS Hild. (*Unio orbiculatus* Hild.).
    Wabash River, Terre Haute; Ohio River.

208. LAMPSILIS ANODONTOIDES Lea. (*Unio teres* Raf.).
    Kankakee, Eel, Tippecanoe, White, Wabash and Ohio rivers.

209. LAMPSILIS FALLACIOSUS Simpson.
    Wabash River, Lafayette; Tippecanoe River, Carroll County.

210. LAMPSILIS RECTUS Lam. (*Unio rectus* Lam.).
    Common in all the rivers of the State.

211. LAMPSILIS SUBROSTRATUS Say. (*Unio subrostratus* Say).
    Wabash, Eel and Ohio rivers; Foote's Pond, Gibson County; Tippecanoe Lake, Kosciusko County; Lake Maxinkuckee, Marshall County; Manitou Lake, Fulton County.

212. LAMPSILIS LIENOSUS Con.
    White River and canal at Indianapolis. Abundant.

213. LAMPSILIS NIGERRIMUS Lea.
    White River, Rockford.

214. LAMPSILIS IRIS Lea. (*Unio iris* Lea).
    All over the State.

215. LAMPSILIS ELLIPSIFORMIS Con. (*Unio spatulatus* Lea).
    Salt Creek, Porter County; Ohio, Wabash and Eel rivers (Call).

216. LAMPSILIS PARVUS Barnes. (*Unio parvus* Barnes).
   White River, Indianapolis; Wabash River, New Harmony; Big Indian Creek, Corydon.

217. LAMPSILIS GLANS Lea. (*Unio glans* Lea).
   White River, Rockford; Tippecanoe Lake, Kosciusko County; Wabash River, New Harmony.

218. LAMPSILIS ALATUS Say. (*Unio alatus* Say).
   Wabash, Ohio, Kankakee and White rivers. Common.

219. LAMPSILIS GRACILIS Barnes. (*Unio gracilis* Barnes).
   Ohio, Wabash, White and Tippecanoe rivers. Common.

220. LAMPSILIS LÆVISSIMUS Lea. (*Unio lævissimus* Lea).
   Wabash River, Terre Haute, Lafayette and New Harmony; Ohio River.

221. LAMPSILIS LEPTODON Raf. (*Unio tenuissimus* Lea).
   Wabash River, New Harmony, Lafayette and Terre Haute.

222. LAMPSILIS BLATCHLEYI Daniels.
   Wabash River, Grand Chain, Posey County.

223. OBOVARIA RETUSA Lam. (*Unio retusus* Lam.).
   White River, Indianapolis, Rockford; Wabash River, Lafayette, Terre Haute, New Harmony.

224. OBOVARIA CIRCULUS Lea. (*Unio circulus* Lea).
   Ohio, Wabash, Tippecanoe, White and Eel rivers.

225. OBOVARIA LENS Lea.
   Ohio, Wabash, Tippecanoe, White and Eel rivers.

226. OBOVARIA ELLIPSIS Lea. (*Unio ellipsis* Lea).
   Wabash River, Lafayette, Terre Haute, New Harmony; Ohio River, New Albany.

227. PLAGIOLA SECURIS Lea. (*Unio lincolatus* Raf.).
   Wabash River, Lafayette, Terre Haute, New Harmony, Grand Chain; Ohio River, New Albany.

228. PLAGIOLA ELEGANS Lea. (*Unio elegans* Lea).
   Ohio, Wabash, Tippecanoe, White and Kankakee rivers.

229. PLAGIOLA DONACIFORMIS Lea. (*Unio donaciformis* Lea).
   Ohio, Wabash, White and Tippecanoe rivers.

230. TRITOGONIA TUBERCULATUS Barnes. (*Unio tuberculatus* Barnes).
   Common in the Ohio and lower Wabash rivers; White River, Rockford; Blue River, Crawford County.

231. CYPROGENIA IRRORATA Lea. (*Unio irroratus* Lea).
   Ohio, Wabash and White rivers. Common.

232. OBLIQUARIA REFLEXA Raf. (*Unio cornutus* Raf.).
   Common in the Ohio, Wabash and White rivers.

233. PTYCHOBRANCHUS PHASEOLUS Hild. (*Unio phaseolus* Hild.).
   Ohio, Wabash, Tippecanoe and White rivers; Tippecanoe Lake, Kosciusko County.

234. STROPHITUS EDENTULUS Say. (*Anodonta edentula* Say; *A. wardiana* Lea).
   Common in all the larger streams in the State; Tippecanoe Lake, Kosciusko County.

234a. S. EDENTULUS PAVONIUS Lea.
   Wabash, Tippecanoe and White rivers; Big Indian River, Corydon.

235. ANODONTA IMBECILLIS Say.
   Ohio, Wabash and White rivers; Lily Lake, Laporte.

236. ANODONTA SUBORBICULATA Say.
   Dan's Pond, Knox County; Foote's Pond, Gibson County, rare; Wier's Lake, Posey County, common; White River, Rockford.

237. ANODONTA GRANDIS Say. (*Anodonta salmonia* Lea).
   Rivers and ponds throughout the State.

237a. A. GRANDIS FOOTIANA Lea.
   Turkey Lake, Kosciusko County; Manitou Lake, Fulton County.

238. ANODONTA CORPULENTA Cooper.
   Clear Lake, Laporte.

239. ANODONTA KENNICOTTII Lea.
   Turkey Lake, Kosciusko County.

240. LASTENA LATA Raf. (*Anodonta dehiscens* Say).
   Ohio, Wabash and Tippecanoe rivers.

241. ANODONTOIDES FERUSSACIANUS Lea.
   Lake Michigan, Millers.

241a. A. FERUSSACIANUS SUBCYLINDRACEUS Lea. (*Anodonta subcylindracea* Lea).
   Wabash River; Berry Lake, Lake County (Baker).

242. ARCIDENS CONFRAGOSUS Say. (*Margaritana confragosa* Say).
   Wabash River, Lafayette, Terre Haute and New Harmony; ponds in Posey County.

243. SYMPHYNOTA COMPRESSA Lea. (*Unio pressus* Lea).
   Wabash, White and Tippecanoe rivers.

244. SYMPHYNOTA COSTATA Raf. (*Margaritana rugosa* Barnes).
   Wabash, Ohio, White, Tippecanoe, Blue, Kankakee and Eel rivers.

245. SYMPHYNOTA COMPLANATA Barnes. (*Margaritana complanata* Barnes).
   Common in all the rivers of the State.

246. ALASMIDONTA CALCEOLA Lea. (*Margaritana deltoidea* Lea).
   Lake Maxinkuckee, Marshall County; Moots Creek, White County; Big Indian River, Harrison County; Salt Creek, Porter County; Wolf Lake (Baker).

247. ALASMIDONTA TRUNCATA B. H. Wright. (*Margaritana marginata* Say).
   In nearly all of the rivers and several of the lakes and ponds.

248. HEMILASTENA AMBIGUA Say. (*Margaritana hildrethiana* Lea).
   Wabash River, Grand Chain, Posey County; White River, Rockford.

249. MARGARITANA MONODONTA Say.
   Grand Chain, Posey County; Falls of the Ohio near New Albany (Call).

250. UNIO GIBBOSUS Barnes.
   Common in the larger streams of the State; Turkey and Tippecanoe lakes, Kosciusko County; Lake Maxinkuckee, Marshall County.

251. UNIO CRASSIDENS Lam.
   Ohio, Wabash and Tippecanoe rivers.

252. UNIO TETRALASMUS Say.
   Ohio and Wabash rivers (Call).

252a. U. TETRALASMUS SAYI Ward.
   Montour's Pond, Knox County.

253. PLEUROBEMA CLAVA Lam. (*Unio clavus* Lam.).

Wabash River, Lafayette, Terre Haute, New Harmony; Tippecanoe River.

254. PLEUROBEMA ÆSOPUS Green. (*Unio cyphyus* Raf.).

Tippecanoe River, Monticello; Wabash River, Lafayette, Terre Haute and New Harmony; Ohio River, New Albany.

255. PLEUROBEMA CICATRICOSA Say. (*Unio varicosus* Lea).

Wabash River.

255a. QUADRULA PLICATA Say.* (*Unio plicatus* Le Sueur).

Common in the Ohio and lower Wabash rivers.

256. QUADRULA UNDULATA Barnes.

Ohio, Wabash, White, Eel, Blue and Tippecanoe rivers.

257. QUADRULA HEROS Say. (*Unio multiplicatus* Say).

Wabash River, Lafayette, Terre Haute, New Harmony; Ohio River, Mt. Vernon.

258. QUADRULA CYLINDRICUS Say. (*Unio cylindricus* Say).

Common in the Ohio, Wabash, White, Eel and Tippecanoe rivers.

259. QUADRULA METANEVRA Raf. (*Unio metanevrus* Raf.).

Ohio, Wabash, White and Blue rivers.

260. Q. METANEVRA WARDII Lea.

Wabash River.

261. QUADRULA LACHRYMOSA Lea. (*Unio lachrymosus* Lea).

Wabash River, Terre Haute and New Harmony; Ohio River.

262. QUADRULA FRAGOSA Conrad. (*Unio fragosus* Conrad).

Wabash River, Gibson County.

263. QUADRULA PUSTULOSA Lea. (*Unio pustulosus* Lea).

Common in the Ohio, Wabash, White and Tippecanoe rivers.

264. QUADRULA COOPERIANA Lea. (*Unio cooperianus* Lea).

Wabash River.

265. QUADRULA PUSTULATA Lea. (*Unio pustulatus* Lea).

Wabash River, Terre Haute and New Harmony; Ohio River, Mt. Vernon.

---

*This is not a variety of *Pleurobema cicatricosa* Say. The number was accidentally omitted in the text, and the number 255a has been given it for that reason.

Printed by Libri Plureos GmbH in Hamburg, Germany